CONVENTION BETWEEN
THE GOVERNMENT OF THE UNITED STATES OF AMERICA AND THE
GOVERNMENT OF THE UNITED KINGDOM
OF GREAT BRITAIN AND NORTHERN IRELAND
FOR THE AVOIDANCE OF DOUBLE TAXATION AND THE
PREVENTION OF FISCAL EVASION
WITH RESPECT TO TAXES ON INCOME AND ON CAPITAL GAINS

The Government of the United States of America and the Government of the United

Kingdom of Great Britain and Northern Ireland,

Desiring to conclude a new Convention for the avoidance of double taxation and the

prevention of fiscal evasion with respect to taxes on income and on capital gains,

Have agreed as follows:

ARTICLE 1

General Scope

1. Except as specifically provided herein, this Convention is applicable only to persons who are residents of one or both of the Contracting States.

2. This Convention shall not restrict in any manner any benefit now or hereafter accorded:

    a) by the laws of either Contracting State; or

    b) by any other agreement between the Contracting States.

3.   a) Notwithstanding the provisions of sub-paragraph b) of paragraph 2 of this Article:

      (i) any question arising as to the interpretation or application of this Convention and, in particular, whether a taxation measure is within the scope of this Convention, shall be determined exclusively in accordance with the provisions of Article 26 (Mutual Agreement Procedure) of this Convention; and

      (ii) the provisions of Article II and Article XVII of the General Agreement on Trade in Services shall not apply to a taxation measure unless the competent authorities agree that the measure is not within the scope of Article 25 (Non-discrimination) of this Convention.

    b) For the purposes of this paragraph, a "measure" is a law, regulation, rule, procedure, decision, administrative action, or any similar provision or action.

4. Notwithstanding any provision of this Convention except paragraph 5 of this Article, a Contracting State may tax its residents (as determined under Article 4 (Residence)), and by reason of citizenship may tax its citizens, as if this Convention had not come into effect.

5. The provisions of paragraph 4 of this Article shall not affect:

    a) the benefits conferred by a Contracting State under paragraph 2 of Article 9 (Associated Enterprises), sub-paragraph b) of paragraph 1 and paragraphs 3 and 5 of Article 17 (Pensions, Social Security, Annuities, Alimony, and Child Support), paragraph 1 of Article 18 (Pension Schemes) and Articles 24 (Relief From Double Taxation), 25 (Non-discrimination), and 26 (Mutual Agreement Procedure) of this Convention; and

    b) the benefits conferred by a Contracting State under paragraph 2 of Article 18 (Pension Schemes) and Articles 19 (Government Service), 20 (Students), and 28 (Diplomatic Agents and Consular Officers) of this Convention, upon individuals who are neither citizens of, nor have been admitted for permanent residence in, that State.

6. A former citizen or long-term resident whose loss of citizenship or long-term resident status had as one of its principal purposes the avoidance of tax (as defined under the laws of the Contracting State of which the person was a citizen or long-term resident) shall be

treated for the purposes of paragraph 4 of this Article as a citizen of that Contracting State but only for a period of 10 years following the loss of such status. This paragraph shall apply only in respect of income from sources within that Contracting State (including income deemed under the domestic law of that State to arise from such sources). Paragraph 4 of this Article shall not apply in the case of any former citizen or long-term resident of a Contracting State who ceased to be a citizen or long-term resident of that State at any time before February 6th, 1995.

7. Where under any provision of this Convention income or gains arising in one of the Contracting States are relieved from tax in that Contracting State and, under the law in force in the other Contracting State, a person, in respect of the said income or gains, is subject to tax by reference to the amount thereof which is remitted to or received in that other Contracting State and not by reference to the full amount thereof, then the relief to be allowed under this Convention in the first-mentioned Contracting State shall apply only to so much of the income or gains as is taxed in the other Contracting State.

8. An item of income, profit or gain derived through a person that is fiscally transparent under the laws of either Contracting State shall be considered to be derived by a resident of a Contracting State to the extent that the item is treated for the purposes of the taxation law of such Contracting State as the income, profit or gain of a resident.

ARTICLE 2
Taxes Covered

1. This Convention shall apply to taxes on income and on capital gains imposed on behalf of a Contracting State irrespective of the manner in which they are levied.

2. There shall be regarded as taxes on income and on capital gains all taxes imposed on total income, or on elements of income, including taxes on gains from the alienation of property.

3. The existing taxes to which this Convention shall apply are:

a) in the case of the United States:

(i) the Federal income taxes imposed by the Internal Revenue Code (but excluding social security taxes); and

(ii) the Federal excise taxes imposed on insurance policies issued by foreign insurers and with respect to private foundations;

b) in the case of the United Kingdom:

(i) the income tax;

(ii) the capital gains tax;

(iii) the corporation tax; and

(iv) the petroleum revenue tax.

4. This Convention shall apply also to any identical or substantially similar taxes that are imposed after the date of signature of this Convention in addition to, or in place of, the existing taxes. The competent authorities of the Contracting States shall notify each other of any changes that have been made in their respective taxation or other laws that significantly affect their obligations under this Convention.

ARTICLE 3
General Definitions

1. For the purposes of this Convention, unless the context otherwise requires:

a) the term "person" includes an individual, an estate, a trust, a partnership, a company, and any other body of persons;

b) the term "company" means any body corporate or any entity that is treated as a body corporate for tax purposes;

c) the term "enterprise" applies to the carrying on of any business;

d) the term "business" includes the performance of professional services and of other activities of an independent character;

e) the terms "enterprise of a Contracting State" and "enterprise of the other Contracting State" mean respectively an enterprise carried on by a resident of a Contracting State, and an enterprise carried on by a resident of the other Contracting State;

f) the term "international traffic" means any transport by a ship or aircraft, except when the ship or aircraft is operated solely between places in the other Contracting State;

g) the term "competent authority" means:

(i) in the United States: the Secretary of the Treasury or his delegate; and

(ii) in the United Kingdom: the Commissioners of Inland Revenue or their authorised representative;

h) the term "United States" means the United States of America, and includes the states thereof and the District of Columbia; such term also includes the territorial sea thereof and the sea bed and sub-soil of the submarine areas adjacent to that territorial sea, over which the United States exercises sovereign rights in accordance with international law; the term, however, does not include Puerto Rico, the Virgin Islands, Guam or any other United States possession or territory;

i) the term "United Kingdom" means Great Britain and Northern Ireland, including any area outside the territorial sea of the United Kingdom which in accordance with international law has been or may hereafter be designated, under the laws of the United Kingdom concerning the Continental Shelf, as an area within which the rights of the United Kingdom with respect to the sea bed and sub-soil and their natural resources may be exercised;

    j) the term "national" of a Contracting State, means:

        (i) in relation to the United States,

            A) any individual possessing the citizenship of the United States; and

            B) any legal person, partnership, association or other entity deriving its status as such from the laws in force in the United States;

        (ii) in relation to the United Kingdom,

            A) any British citizen, or any British subject not possessing the citizenship of any other Commonwealth country or territory, provided he has the right of abode in the United Kingdom; and

            B) any legal person, partnership, association or other entity deriving its status as such from the laws in force in the United Kingdom;

    k) the term "qualified governmental entity" means:

        (i) a Contracting State, or a political subdivision or local authority of a Contracting State;

        (ii) a person that is wholly owned, directly or indirectly, by a Contracting State or a political subdivision or local authority of a Contracting State, provided

            A) it is organized under the laws of the Contracting State;

            B) its earnings are credited to its own account with no portion of its income inuring to the benefit of any private person;

            C) its assets vest in the Contracting State, political subdivision or local authority upon dissolution; and

            D) it does not carry on a business;

    l) the term "Contracting State" means the United States or the United Kingdom, as the context requires;

    m) the term "real property" means any interest (other than an interest solely as a creditor) in land, crops or timber growing on land, mines, wells and other places of extraction of natural resources, as well as any fixture built on land (buildings, structures, etc.) and other property considered real or immovable property under the law of the Contracting State in which the property in question is situated. The term shall in any case include livestock and equipment used in agriculture and forestry, rights to which the provisions of general law respecting landed property apply, usufruct of real property and rights to variable or fixed payments as consideration for the working of, or the right to work, mineral deposits and other natural resources; ships, boats and aircraft shall not be regarded as real property.

n) the term "conduit arrangement" means a transaction or series of transactions:

(i) which is structured in such a way that a resident of a Contracting State entitled to the benefits of this Convention receives an item of income arising in the other Contracting State but that resident pays, directly or indirectly, all or substantially all of that income (at any time or in any form) to another person who is not a resident of either Contracting State and who, if it received that item of income direct from the other Contracting State, would not be entitled under a convention for the avoidance of double taxation between the state in which that other person is resident and the Contracting State in which the income arises, or otherwise, to benefits with respect to that item of income which are equivalent to, or more favourable than, those available under this Convention to a resident of a Contracting State; and

(ii) which has as its main purpose, or one of its main purposes, obtaining such increased benefits as are available under this Convention.

o) the term "pension scheme" means any plan, scheme, fund, trust or other arrangement established in a Contracting State which is:

(i) generally exempt from income taxation in that State; and

(ii) operated principally to administer or provide pension or retirement benefits or to earn income for the benefit of one or more such arrangements.

2. As regards the application of this Convention at any time by a Contracting State, any term not defined therein shall, unless the context otherwise requires, or the competent authorities agree on a common meaning pursuant to the provisions of Article 26 (Mutual Agreement Procedure) of this Convention, have the meaning which it has at that time under the law of that State for the purposes of the taxes to which this Convention applies, any meaning under the applicable tax laws of that State prevailing over a meaning given to the term under other laws of that State.

ARTICLE 4
Residence

1. Except as provided in paragraphs 2 and 3 of this Article, the term "resident of a Contracting State" means, for the purposes of this Convention, any person who, under the laws of that State, is liable to tax therein by reason of his domicile, residence, citizenship, place of management, place of incorporation, or any other criterion of a similar nature. This term, however, does not include any person who is liable to tax in that State in respect only of income from sources in that State or of profits attributable to a permanent establishment in that State.

2. An individual who is a United States citizen or an alien admitted to the United States for permanent residence (a "green card" holder) is a resident of the United States only if the individual has a substantial presence, permanent home or habitual abode in the United States and if that individual is not a resident of a State other than the United Kingdom for the purposes of a double taxation convention between that State and the United Kingdom.

3. The term "resident of a Contracting State" includes:

a) a pension scheme;

b) a plan, scheme, fund, trust, company or other arrangement established in a Contracting State that is operated exclusively to administer or provide employee benefits and that, by reason of its nature as such, is generally exempt from income taxation in that State;

c) an organization that is established exclusively for religious, charitable, scientific, artistic, cultural, or educational purposes and that is a resident of a Contracting State according to its laws, notwithstanding that all or part of its income or gains may be exempt from tax under the domestic law of that State; and

d) a qualified governmental entity that is, is a part of, or is established in, that State.

4. Where by reason of the provisions of paragraph 1 of this Article, an individual is a resident of both Contracting States, then his status shall be determined as follows:

a) he shall be deemed to be a resident only of the State in which he has a permanent home available to him; if he has a permanent home available to him in both States, he shall be deemed to be a resident only of the State with which his personal and economic relations are closer (centre of vital interests);

b) if the State in which he has his centre of vital interests cannot be determined, or if he does not have a permanent home available to him in either State, he shall be deemed to be a resident only of the State in which he has an habitual abode;

c) if he has an habitual abode in both States or in neither of them, he shall be deemed to be a resident only of the State of which he is a national;

d) if he is a national of both States or of neither of them, the competent authorities of the Contracting States shall endeavour to settle the question by mutual agreement.

5. Where by reason of the provisions of paragraph 1 of this Article a person other than an individual is a resident of both Contracting States, the competent authorities of the Contracting States shall endeavour to determine by mutual agreement the mode of application of this Convention to that person. If the competent authorities do not reach such an agreement, that person shall not be entitled to claim any benefit provided by this Convention, except those

provided by paragraph 4 of Article 24 (Relief from Double Taxation), Article 25 (Non-discrimination) and Article 26 (Mutual Agreement Procedure).

6. A marriage before January 1st, 1974 between a woman who is a United States national and a man domiciled within the United Kingdom shall be deemed to have taken place on January 1st, 1974 for the purpose of determining her domicile for United Kingdom tax purposes, on or after the date on which this Convention first has effect in relation to her.

ARTICLE 5
Permanent Establishment

1. For the purposes of this Convention, the term "permanent establishment" means a fixed place of business through which the business of an enterprise is wholly or partly carried on.

2. The term "permanent establishment" includes especially:

    a) a place of management;

    b) a branch;

    c) an office;

    d) a factory;

    e) a workshop; and

    f) a mine, an oil or gas well, a quarry, or any other place of extraction of natural resources.

3. A building site or construction or installation project constitutes a permanent establishment only if it lasts for more than twelve months.

4. Notwithstanding the preceding provisions of this Article, the term "permanent establishment" shall be deemed not to include:

    a) the use of facilities solely for the purpose of storage, display or delivery of goods or merchandise belonging to the enterprise;

    b) the maintenance of a stock of goods or merchandise belonging to the enterprise solely for the purpose of storage, display or delivery;

    c) the maintenance of a stock of goods or merchandise belonging to the enterprise solely for the purpose of processing by another enterprise;

    d) the maintenance of a fixed place of business solely for the purpose of purchasing goods or merchandise, or of collecting information, for the enterprise;

    e) the maintenance of a fixed place of business solely for the purpose of carrying on, for the enterprise, any other activity of a preparatory or auxiliary character;

    f) the maintenance of a fixed place of business solely for any combination of the activities mentioned in sub-paragraphs a) to e) of this paragraph, provided that the overall activity of the fixed place of business resulting from this combination is of a preparatory or auxiliary character.

5. Notwithstanding the provisions of paragraphs 1 and 2 of this Article, where a person - other than an agent of an independent status to whom paragraph 6 of this Article applies - is acting on behalf of an enterprise and has and habitually exercises in a Contracting State an authority to conclude contracts that are binding on the enterprise, that enterprise shall be deemed to have a permanent establishment in that State in respect of any activities that the person undertakes for the enterprise, unless the activities of such person are limited to those mentioned in paragraph 4 of this Article that, if exercised through a fixed place of business, would not make this fixed place of business a permanent establishment under the provisions of that paragraph.

6. An enterprise shall not be deemed to have a permanent establishment in a Contracting State merely because it carries on business in that State through a broker, general commission agent, or any other agent of an independent status, provided that such person is acting in the ordinary course of his business as an independent agent.

7. The fact that a company that is a resident of a Contracting State controls or is controlled by a company that is a resident of the other Contracting State, or that carries on business in that other State (whether through a permanent establishment or otherwise), shall not constitute either company a permanent establishment of the other.

ARTICLE 6

Income from Real Property

1. Income derived by a resident of a Contracting State from real property, including income from agriculture or forestry, situated in the other Contracting State may be taxed in that other State.

2. The provisions of paragraph 1 of this Article shall apply to income derived from the direct use, letting, or use in any other form of real property.

3. The provisions of paragraphs 1 and 2 of this Article shall also apply to the income from real property of an enterprise.

ARTICLE 7

Business Profits

1. The business profits of an enterprise of a Contracting State shall be taxable only in that State unless the enterprise carries on business in the other Contracting State through a permanent establishment situated therein. If the enterprise carries on business as aforesaid, the business profits of the enterprise may be taxed in the other State but only so much of them as are attributable to that permanent establishment.

2. Subject to the provisions of paragraph 3 of this Article, where an enterprise of a Contracting State carries on business in the other Contracting State through a permanent establishment situated therein, there shall in each Contracting State be attributed to that permanent establishment the business profits that it might be expected to make if it were a distinct and separate enterprise engaged in the same or similar activities under the same or similar conditions and dealing wholly independently with the enterprise of which it is a permanent establishment. For this purpose, the business profits to be attributed to the permanent establishment shall include only the profits derived from the assets used, risks assumed and activities performed by the permanent establishment.

3. In determining the business profits of a permanent establishment, there shall be allowed as deductions expenses that are incurred for the purposes of the permanent establishment, including executive and general administrative expenses so incurred, whether in the State in which the permanent establishment is situated or elsewhere.

4. For the purposes of the preceding paragraphs, the profits to be attributed to the permanent establishment shall be determined by the same method year by year unless there is good and sufficient reason to the contrary.

5. The United States excise tax on insurance policies issued by foreign insurers shall not be imposed on insurance or reinsurance policies, the premiums on which are the receipts of a business of insurance carried on by an enterprise of the United Kingdom. However, if such policies are entered into as part of a conduit arrangement, the United States may impose excise tax on those policies, unless the premiums in respect of those policies are, or are part of, the income of a permanent establishment that the enterprise of the United Kingdom has in the United States.

6. Where business profits include items of income that are dealt with separately in other Articles of this Convention, then the provisions of those Articles shall not be affected by the provisions of this Article.

7. In applying this Article, paragraph 5 of Article 10 (Dividends), paragraph 3 of Article 11 (Interest), paragraph 3 of Article 12 (Royalties), and paragraph 2 of Article 22 (Other Income) of this Convention, income or profits attributable to a permanent establishment may, notwithstanding that the permanent establishment has ceased to exist, be taxed in the Contracting State in which it was situated.

ARTICLE 8

Shipping and Air Transport

1. Profits of an enterprise of a Contracting State from the operation of ships or aircraft in international traffic shall be taxable only in that State.

2. For the purposes of this Article, profits from the operation of ships or aircraft include profits derived from the rental of ships or aircraft on a full (time or voyage) basis. They also include profits from the rental of ships or aircraft on a bareboat basis if the rental income is incidental to profits from the operation of ships or aircraft in international traffic. Profits derived by an enterprise from the inland transport of property or passengers within either Contracting State shall be treated as profits from the operation of ships or aircraft in international traffic if such transport is undertaken as part of international traffic conducted by such enterprise.

3. Profits of an enterprise of a Contracting State from the use, maintenance, or rental of containers (including trailers, barges and related equipment for the transport of containers) used in international traffic shall be taxable only in that State.

4. The provisions of paragraphs 1 and 3 of this Article shall also apply to profits from participation in a pool, a joint business, or an international operating agency.

ARTICLE 9
Associated Enterprises

1. Where:

a) an enterprise of a Contracting State participates directly or indirectly in the management, control or capital of an enterprise of the other Contracting State; or

b) the same persons participate directly or indirectly in the management, control, or capital of an enterprise of a Contracting State and an enterprise of the other Contracting State,

and in either case conditions are made or imposed between the two enterprises in their commercial or financial relations that differ from those that would be made between independent enterprises, then any profits that, but for those conditions, would have accrued to one of the enterprises, but by reason of those conditions have not so accrued, may be included in the profits of that enterprise and taxed accordingly.

2. Where a Contracting State includes in the profits of an enterprise of that State, and taxes accordingly, profits on which an enterprise of the other Contracting State has been charged to tax in that other State, and the other Contracting State agrees that the profits so included are profits that would have accrued to the enterprise of the first-mentioned State if the conditions made between the two enterprises had been those that would have been made between independent enterprises, then that other State shall make an appropriate adjustment to the amount of the tax charged therein on those profits. In determining such adjustment, due regard shall be paid to the other provisions of this Convention and the competent authorities of the Contracting States shall if necessary consult each other.

ARTICLE 10
Dividends

1. Dividends paid by a company which is a resident of a Contracting State to a resident of the other Contracting State may be taxed in that other State.

2. However, such dividends may also be taxed in the Contracting State of which the company paying the dividends is a resident and according to the laws of that State, but if the dividends are beneficially owned by a resident of the other Contracting State, the tax so charged shall not exceed, except as otherwise provided,

    a) 5 per cent. of the gross amount of the dividends if the beneficial owner is a company that owns shares representing directly or indirectly at least 10 per cent. of the voting power of the company paying the dividends;

    b) 15 per cent. of the gross amount of the dividends in all other cases.

This paragraph shall not affect the taxation of the company in respect of the profits out of which the dividends are paid.

3. Notwithstanding the provisions of paragraph 2 of this Article, dividends shall not be taxed in the Contracting State of which the company paying the dividends is a resident if the beneficial owner of the dividends is a resident of the other Contracting State and either:

    a) a company that has owned shares representing 80 per cent. or more of the voting power of the company paying the dividends for a 12-month period ending on the date the dividend is declared, and that:

        (i) owned shares representing, directly or indirectly, at least 80 per cent. of the voting power of the company paying the dividends prior to October 1st, 1998; or

        (ii) is a qualified person by reason of sub-paragraph c) of paragraph 2 of Article 23 (Limitation on Benefits) of this Convention; or

        (iii) is entitled to benefits with respect to the dividends under paragraph 3 or paragraph 6 of that Article; or

    b) a pension scheme, provided that such dividends are not derived from the carrying on of a business, directly or indirectly, by such pension scheme.

4. Sub-paragraph a) of paragraph 2 and paragraph 3 of this Article shall not apply in the case of dividends paid by a pooled investment vehicle which is a resident of a Contracting State. Sub-paragraph b) of paragraph 2 of this Article shall apply in the case of dividends paid by a pooled investment vehicle, the assets of which consist wholly or mainly of shares, securities or currencies or derivative contracts relating to shares, securities or currencies. In the case of dividends paid by a pooled investment vehicle not described in the preceding sentence, sub-paragraph b) of paragraph 2 of this Article shall apply only if:

a) the beneficial owner of the dividends is an individual holding an interest of not more than 10 per cent. in the pooled investment vehicle;

b) the dividends are paid with respect to a class of stock that is publicly traded and the beneficial owner of the dividends is a person holding an interest of not more than 5 per cent. of any class of the stock of the pooled investment vehicle; or

c) the beneficial owner of the dividends is a person holding an interest of not more than 10 per cent. in the pooled investment vehicle and that vehicle is diversified.

5. The previous provisions of this Article shall not apply if the beneficial owner of the dividends, being a resident of a Contracting State, carries on business in the other Contracting State, of which the payer is a resident, through a permanent establishment situated therein, and the dividends are attributable to such permanent establishment. In such case, the provisions of Article 7 (Business Profits) of this Convention shall apply.

6. A Contracting State may not impose any tax on dividends paid by a company which is a resident of the other Contracting State, except insofar as the dividends are paid to a resident of the first-mentioned State or the dividends are attributable to a permanent establishment situated in that State, nor may it impose tax on a company's undistributed profits, except as provided in paragraph 7 of this Article, even if the dividends paid or the undistributed profits consist wholly or partly of profits or income arising in that State.

7. A company that is a resident of a Contracting State and that has a permanent establishment in the other Contracting State, or that is subject to tax in that other State on a net basis on its income or gains that may be taxed in that other State under Article 6 (Income from Real Property) or under paragraph 1 of Article 13 (Gains) of this Convention, may be subject in that other State to a tax in addition to any tax that may be imposed by that other State in accordance with the other provisions of this Convention. Such tax, however, may be imposed on only the portion of the business profits of the company attributable to the permanent establishment, and the portion of the income or gains referred to in the preceding sentence that is subject to tax under Article 6 or under paragraph 1 of Article 13, that, in the case of the United States, represents the dividend equivalent amount of such profits, income or gains and, in the case of the United Kingdom, is an amount that is analogous to the dividend equivalent amount. This paragraph shall not apply in the case of a company which:

a) prior to October 1st, 1998 was engaged in activities giving rise to profits attributable to that permanent establishment or to income or gains to which the provisions of Article 6 or, as the case may be, paragraph 1 of Article 13 apply;

b) is a qualified person by reason of sub-paragraph c) of paragraph 2 of Article 23 (Limitation on Benefits) of this Convention; or

c) is entitled to benefits under paragraph 3 or paragraph 6 of that Article with respect to an item of income, profit or gain described in this paragraph.

8. The additional tax referred to in paragraph 7 of this Article may not be imposed at a rate in excess of the rate specified in sub-paragraph a) of paragraph 2 of this Article.

9. The provisions of this Article shall not apply in respect of any dividend paid under, or as part of, a conduit arrangement.

10. For the purposes of this Article:

a) the term "dividends" means income from shares or other rights, not being debt-claims, participating in profits, as well as income from other corporate rights and any other item which, under the laws of the Contracting State of which the company paying the dividend is a resident, is treated as a dividend or a distribution of a company;

b) the term "pooled investment vehicle" means a person:

(i) whose assets consist wholly or mainly of real property, or of shares, securities or currencies, or of derivative contracts relating to shares, securities or currencies or real property;

(ii) whose gross income consists wholly or mainly of dividends, interest, gains from the alienation of assets and rents and other income and gains from the holding and alienation of real property; and

(iii) which, in respect of its income, profits or gains, is exempt from, or is not chargeable to, tax in the State of which it is a resident, or is subject to tax at a special rate in that State, or which is entitled to a deduction for dividends paid to its shareholders in computing the amount of its income, profits or gains;

c) a pooled investment vehicle is "diversified" if the value of no single interest in real property exceeds 10 per cent. of the pooled investment vehicle's total interests in real property. For the purposes of this rule, foreclosure property shall not be considered an interest in real property. Where a pooled investment vehicle holds an interest in a partnership, it shall be treated as owning directly a proportion of the partnership's interests in real property corresponding to the proportion of its interest in the partnership.

ARTICLE 11

Interest

1. Interest arising in a Contracting State and beneficially owned by a resident of the other Contracting State shall be taxable only in that other State.

2. The term "interest" as used in this Article means income from debt-claims of every kind, whether or not secured by mortgage, and whether or not carrying a right to participate in the debtor's profits, and, in particular, income from government securities and income from bonds or debentures, including premiums or prizes attaching to such securities, bonds or debentures, and all other income that is subjected to the same taxation treatment as income

from money lent by the taxation law of the Contracting State in which the income arises. Income dealt with in Article 10 (Dividends) of this Convention and penalty charges for late payment shall not be regarded as interest for the purposes of this Article.

3. The provisions of paragraph 1 of this Article shall not apply if the beneficial owner of the interest, being a resident of a Contracting State, carries on business in the other Contracting State, in which the interest arises, through a permanent establishment situated therein, and the interest is attributable to such permanent establishment. In such case, the provisions of Article 7 (Business Profits) of this Convention shall apply.

4. Where, by reason of a special relationship between the payer and the beneficial owner or between both of them and some other person, the amount of the interest exceeds, for whatever reason, the amount which would have been agreed upon by the payer and the beneficial owner in the absence of such relationship, the provisions of this Article shall apply only to the last-mentioned amount. In such case, the excess part of the payments shall remain taxable according to the laws of each State, due regard being had to the other provisions of this Convention.

5.   a) Notwithstanding the provisions of paragraph 1 of this Article, interest paid by a resident of a Contracting State and determined by reference to receipts, sales, income, profits or other cash flow of the debtor or a related person, to any change in the value of any property of the debtor or a related person or to any dividend, partnership distribution or similar payment made by the debtor to a related person, may also be taxed in the Contracting State in which it arises, and according to the laws of that State, but if the beneficial owner is a resident of the other Contracting State the gross amount of the interest may be taxed at a rate not exceeding the rate prescribed in sub-paragraph b) of paragraph 2 of Article 10 (Dividends) of this Convention.

b) Sub-paragraph a) of this paragraph shall not apply to any interest solely by reason of the fact that it is paid under an arrangement the terms of which provide:

(i) that the amount of interest payable shall be reduced in the event of an improvement in the factors by reference to which the amount of interest payable is determined; or

(ii) that the amount of interest payable shall be increased in the event of a deterioration in the factors by reference to which the amount of interest payable is determined.

6. Notwithstanding the provisions of paragraph 1 of this Article, a Contracting State may tax, in accordance with its domestic law, interest paid with respect to the ownership interests in a vehicle used for the securitisation of real estate mortgages or other assets, to the extent that the amount of interest paid exceeds the return on comparable debt instruments as specified by the domestic law of that State.

7. The provisions of this Article shall not apply in respect of any interest paid under, or as part of, a conduit arrangement.

ARTICLE 12
Royalties

1. Royalties arising in a Contracting State and beneficially owned by a resident of the other Contracting State shall be taxable only in that other State.

2. The term "royalties" as used in this Article means:

    a) any consideration for the use of, or the right to use, any copyright of literary, artistic, scientific or other work (including computer software and cinematographic films) including works reproduced on audio or video tapes or disks or any other means of image or sound reproduction, any patent, trade mark, design or model, plan, secret formula or process, or other like right or property, or for information concerning industrial, commercial or scientific experience; and

    b) any gain derived from the alienation of any right or property described in sub-paragraph a) of this paragraph, to the extent that the amount of such gain is contingent on the productivity, use, or disposition of the right or property.

3. The provisions of paragraph 1 of this Article shall not apply if the beneficial owner of the royalties, being a resident of a Contracting State, carries on business in the other Contracting State, in which the royalties arise, through a permanent establishment situated therein, and the royalties are attributable to such permanent establishment. In such case, the provisions of Article 7 (Business Profits) of this Convention shall apply.

4. Where, by reason of a special relationship between the payer and the beneficial owner or between both of them and some other person, the amount of the royalties paid exceeds, for whatever reason, the amount which would have been agreed upon by the payer and the beneficial owner in the absence of such relationship, the provisions of this Article shall apply only to the last-mentioned amount. In such case, the excess part of the payments shall remain taxable according to the laws of each Contracting State, due regard being had to the other provisions of this Convention.

5. The provisions of this Article shall not apply in respect of any royalty paid under, or as part of, a conduit arrangement.

ARTICLE 13
Gains

1. Gains derived by a resident of a Contracting State that are attributable to the alienation of real property situated in the other Contracting State may be taxed in that other State.

2. For the purposes of this Article the term "real property situated in the other Contracting State" shall include:

a) rights to assets to be produced by the exploration or exploitation of the sea bed and sub-soil of that other State and their natural resources, including rights to interests in or the benefit of such assets;

b) where that other State is the United States, a United States real property interest; and

c) where that other State is the United Kingdom:

(i) shares, including rights to acquire shares, other than shares in which there is regular trading on a stock exchange, deriving their value or the greater part of their value directly or indirectly from real property situated in the United Kingdom; and

(ii) an interest in a partnership or trust to the extent that the assets of the partnership or trust consist of real property situated in the United Kingdom, or of shares referred to in clause (i) of this sub-paragraph.

3. Gains from the alienation of property (other than real property) forming part of the business property of a permanent establishment that an enterprise of a Contracting State has or had in the other Contracting State, including gains from the alienation of such a permanent establishment (alone or with the whole enterprise), may be taxed in that other State, whether or not that permanent establishment exists at the time of the alienation.

4. Gains derived by an enterprise of a Contracting State from the alienation of ships or aircraft operated in international traffic by the enterprise, or of containers used in international traffic, or of property (other than real property) pertaining to the operation or use of such ships, aircraft or containers, shall be taxable only in that State.

5. Gains from the alienation of any property other than property referred to in the preceding paragraphs of this Article shall be taxable only in the Contracting State of which the alienator is a resident.

6. The provisions of paragraph 5 of this Article shall not affect the right of a Contracting State to levy according to its law a tax on gains from the alienation of any property derived by an individual who is a resident of the other Contracting State and has been a resident of the first-mentioned Contracting State at any time during the six years immediately preceding the alienation of the property.

ARTICLE 14

Income from Employment

1. Subject to the provisions of Articles 15 (Directors' Fees), 17 (Pensions, Social Security, Annuities, Alimony, and Child Support) and 19 (Government Service) of this

Convention, salaries, wages, and other similar remuneration derived by a resident of a Contracting State in respect of an employment shall be taxable only in that State unless the employment is exercised in the other Contracting State. If the employment is so exercised, such remuneration as is derived therefrom may be taxed in that other State.

2. Notwithstanding the provisions of paragraph 1 of this Article, remuneration derived by a resident of a Contracting State in respect of an employment exercised in the other Contracting State shall be taxable only in the first-mentioned State if:

a) the recipient is present in the other State for a period or periods not exceeding in the aggregate 183 days in any twelve-month period commencing or ending in the taxable year or year of assessment concerned;

b) the remuneration is paid by, or on behalf of, an employer who is not a resident of the other State; and

c) the remuneration is not borne by a permanent establishment which the employer has in the other State.

3. Notwithstanding the preceding provisions of this Article, remuneration described in paragraph 1 of this Article that is derived by a resident of a Contracting State in respect of an employment as a member of the regular complement of a ship or aircraft operated in international traffic shall be taxable only in that State.

ARTICLE 15

Directors' Fees

Directors' fees and other similar payments derived by a resident of a Contracting State for services rendered in the other Contracting State in his capacity as a member of the board of directors of a company that is a resident of the other Contracting State may be taxed in that other State.

ARTICLE 16

Entertainers and Sportsmen

1. Income derived by a resident of a Contracting State as an entertainer, such as a theatre, motion picture, radio, or television artiste, or a musician, or as a sportsman, from his personal activities as such exercised in the other Contracting State, which income would be exempt from tax in that other State under the provisions of Article 7 (Business Profits) or 14 (Income from Employment) of this Convention, may be taxed in that other State, except where the amount of the gross receipts derived by that resident, including expenses reimbursed to him or borne on his behalf, from such activities does not exceed twenty thousand United States dollars ($20,000) or its equivalent in pounds sterling for the taxable year or year of assessment concerned.

2. Income in respect of activities exercised by an entertainer or a sportsman in his capacity as such which accrues not to the entertainer or sportsman himself but to another person may, notwithstanding the provisions of Article 7 (Business Profits) or 14 (Income from Employment) of this Convention, be taxed in the Contracting State in which the activities of the entertainer or sportsman are exercised, unless that other person establishes that neither the entertainer or sportsman nor persons related thereto participate directly or indirectly in the profits of that other person in any manner, including the receipt of deferred remuneration, bonuses, fees, dividends, partnership distributions, or other distributions.

ARTICLE 17
Pensions, Social Security, Annuities, Alimony, and Child Support

1.   a) Pensions and other similar remuneration beneficially owned by a resident of a Contracting State shall be taxable only in that State.

b) Notwithstanding sub-paragraph a) of this paragraph, the amount of any such pension or remuneration paid from a pension scheme established in the other Contracting State that would be exempt from taxation in that other State if the beneficial owner were a resident thereof shall be exempt from taxation in the first-mentioned State.

2. Notwithstanding the provisions of paragraph 1 of this Article, a lump-sum payment derived from a pension scheme established in a Contracting State and beneficially owned by a resident of the other Contracting State shall be taxable only in the first-mentioned State.

3. Notwithstanding the provisions of paragraph 1 of this Article, payments made by a Contracting State under the provisions of the social security or similar legislation of that State to a resident of the other Contracting State shall be taxable only in that other State.

4. Any annuity derived and beneficially owned by an individual ("the annuitant") who is a resident of a Contracting State shall be taxable only in that State. The term "annuity" as used in this paragraph means a stated sum paid periodically at stated times during the life of the annuitant, or during a specified or ascertainable period of time, under an obligation to make the payments in return for adequate and full consideration (other than in return for services rendered).

5. Periodic payments, made pursuant to a written separation agreement or a decree of divorce, separate maintenance, or compulsory support, including payments for the support of a child, paid by a resident of a Contracting State to a resident of the other Contracting State, shall be exempt from tax in both Contracting States, except that, if the payer is entitled to relief from tax for such payments in the first-mentioned State, such payments shall be taxable only in the other State.

ARTICLE 18
Pension Schemes

1. Where an individual who is a resident of a Contracting State is a member or beneficiary of, or participant in, a pension scheme established in the other Contracting State, income earned by the pension scheme may be taxed as income of that individual only when, and, subject to paragraphs 1 and 2 of Article 17 (Pensions, Social Security, Annuities, Alimony, and Child Support) of this Convention, to the extent that, it is paid to, or for the benefit of, that individual from the pension scheme (and not transferred to another pension scheme).

2. Where an individual who is a member or beneficiary of, or participant in, a pension scheme established in a Contracting State exercises an employment or self-employment in the other Contracting State:

> a) contributions paid by or on behalf of that individual to the pension scheme during the period that he exercises an employment or self-employment in the other State shall be deductible (or excludable) in computing his taxable income in that other State; and

> b) any benefits accrued under the pension scheme, or contributions made to the pension scheme by or on behalf of the individual's employer, during that period shall not be treated as part of the employee's taxable income and any such contributions shall be allowed as a deduction in computing the business profits of his employer in that other State.

The reliefs available under this paragraph shall not exceed the reliefs that would be allowed by the other State to residents of that State for contributions to, or benefits accrued under, a pension scheme established in that State.

3. The provisions of paragraph 2 of this Article shall not apply unless:

> a) contributions by or on behalf of the individual, or by or on behalf of the individual's employer, to the pension scheme (or to another similar pension scheme for which the first-mentioned pension scheme was substituted) were made before the individual began to exercise an employment or self-employment in the other State; and

> b) the competent authority of the other State has agreed that the pension scheme generally corresponds to a pension scheme established in that other State.

4. Where, under sub-paragraph a) of paragraph 2 of this Article, contributions to a pension scheme are deductible (or excludable) in computing an individual's taxable income in a Contracting State and, under the laws in force in that State, the individual is subject to tax in that State, in respect of income, profits or gains, by reference to the amount thereof which is remitted to or received in that State and not by reference to the full amount thereof, then the relief that would otherwise be available to that individual under that sub-paragraph in respect of such contributions shall be reduced to an amount that bears the same proportion to that relief as

the amount of the income, profits or gains in respect of which the individual is subject to tax in that State bears to the amount of the income, profits or gains in respect of which he would be subject to tax if he were so subject in respect of the full amount thereof and not only in respect of the amount remitted to or received in that State.

5.   a) Where a citizen of the United States who is a resident of the United Kingdom exercises an employment in the United Kingdom the income from which is taxable in the United Kingdom and is borne by an employer who is a resident of the United Kingdom or by a permanent establishment situated in the United Kingdom, and the individual is a member or beneficiary of, or participant in, a pension scheme established in the United Kingdom,

(i) contributions paid by or on behalf of that individual to the pension scheme during the period that he exercises the employment in the United Kingdom, and that are attributable to the employment, shall be deductible (or excludable) in computing his taxable income in the United States; and

(ii) any benefits accrued under the pension scheme, or contributions made to the pension scheme by or on behalf of the individual's employer, during that period, and that are attributable to the employment, shall not be treated as part of the employee's taxable income in computing his taxable income in the United States.

This paragraph shall apply only to the extent that the contributions or benefits qualify for tax relief in the United Kingdom.

b) The reliefs available under this paragraph shall not exceed the reliefs that would be allowed by the United States to its residents for contributions to, or benefits accrued under, a generally corresponding pension scheme established in the United States.

c) For purposes of determining an individual's eligibility to participate in and receive tax benefits with respect to a pension scheme established in the United States, contributions made to, or benefits accrued under, a pension scheme established in the United Kingdom shall be treated as contributions or benefits under a generally corresponding pension scheme established in the United States to the extent reliefs are available to the individual under this paragraph.

d) This paragraph shall not apply unless the competent authority of the United States has agreed that the pension scheme generally corresponds to a pension scheme established in the United States.

ARTICLE 19

Government Service

1. Notwithstanding the provisions of Articles 14 (Income from Employment), 15 (Directors' Fees) and 16 (Entertainers and Sportsmen) of this Convention:

a) salaries, wages and other similar remuneration, other than a pension, paid from the public funds of a Contracting State or a political subdivision or a local authority thereof to an individual in respect of services rendered to that State or subdivision or authority shall, subject to the provisions of sub-paragraph b) of this paragraph, be taxable only in that State;

b) such salaries, wages and other similar remuneration, however, shall be taxable only in the other Contracting State if the services are rendered in that State and the individual is a resident of that State who:

(i) is a national of that State; or

(ii) did not become a resident of that State solely for the purpose of rendering the services.

2. Notwithstanding the provisions of paragraphs 1 and 2 of Article 17 (Pensions, Social Security, Annuities, Alimony, and Child Support) of this Convention:

a) any pension paid by, or out of funds created by, a Contracting State or a political subdivision or a local authority thereof to an individual in respect of services rendered to that State or subdivision or authority shall, subject to the provisions of sub-paragraph b) of this paragraph, be taxable only in that State;

b) such pension, however, shall be taxable only in the other Contracting State if the individual is a resident of, and a national of, that State.

3. The provisions of Articles 14 (Income from Employment), 15 (Directors' Fees), 16 (Entertainers and Sportsmen) and 17 (Pensions, Social Security, Annuities, Alimony, and Child Support) of this Convention shall apply to salaries, wages and other similar remuneration, and to pensions, in respect of services rendered in connection with a business carried on by a Contracting State or a political subdivision or a local authority thereof.

ARTICLE 20

Students

Payments received by a student or business apprentice who is, or was immediately before visiting a Contracting State, a resident of the other Contracting State, and who is present in the first-mentioned State for the purpose of his full-time education at a university, college or other recognised educational institution of a similar nature, or for his full-time training, shall not be taxed in that State, provided that such payments arise outside that State, and are for the purpose of his maintenance, education or training. The exemption from tax provided by this

Article shall apply to a business apprentice only for a period of time not exceeding one year from the date he first arrives in the first-mentioned Contracting State for the purpose of his training.

ARTICLE 21
Offshore Exploration and Exploitation Activities

1. The provisions of this Article shall apply notwithstanding any other provision of this Convention where activities are carried on offshore in a Contracting State in connection with the exploration (hereinafter called "exploration activities") or exploitation (hereinafter called "exploitation activities") of the sea bed and sub-soil and their natural resources situated in that State.

2. An enterprise of a Contracting State which carries on exploration activities or exploitation activities in the other Contracting State shall, subject to paragraph 3 of this Article, be deemed to be carrying on business in that other State through a permanent establishment situated therein.

3. Exploration activities which are carried on by an enterprise of a Contracting State in the other Contracting State for a period or periods not exceeding in the aggregate 30 days within any period of twelve months shall not constitute the carrying on of business through a permanent establishment situated therein. For the purposes of determining such period or periods:

a) where an enterprise of a Contracting State carrying on exploration activities in the other Contracting State is associated with another enterprise carrying on substantially similar exploration activities there, the former enterprise shall be deemed to be carrying on all such activities of the latter enterprise, except to the extent that those activities are carried on at the same time as its own activities;

b) an enterprise shall be regarded as associated with another enterprise if one participates directly or indirectly in the management, control or capital of the other or if the same persons participate directly or indirectly in the management, control or capital of both enterprises.

4. Salaries, wages and other similar remuneration derived by a resident of a Contracting State from an employment in respect of exploration activities or exploitation activities carried on in the other Contracting State may be taxed in that other State, to the extent that the duties are performed offshore in that other State. However, income derived by a resident of a Contracting State in respect of such employment performed in the other Contracting State shall not be taxable in that other State if the employment is performed in that other State for a period or periods not exceeding in the aggregate 30 days within any period of twelve months.

ARTICLE 22
Other Income

1. Items of income beneficially owned by a resident of a Contracting State, wherever arising, not dealt with in the foregoing Articles of this Convention (other than income paid out of trusts or the estates of deceased persons in the course of administration) shall be taxable only in that State.

2. The provisions of paragraph 1 of this Article shall not apply to income, other than income from real property, if the beneficial owner of the income, being a resident of a Contracting State, carries on business in the other Contracting State through a permanent establishment situated therein, and the income is attributable to such permanent establishment. In such case, the provisions of Article 7 (Business Profits) of this Convention shall apply.

3. Where, by reason of a special relationship between the resident referred to in paragraph 1 of this Article and some other person, or between both of them and some third person, the amount of the income referred to in that paragraph exceeds the amount (if any) which would have been agreed upon between them in the absence of such relationship, the provisions of this Article shall apply only to the last-mentioned amount. In such a case, the excess part of the income shall remain taxable according to the laws of each Contracting State, due regard being had to the other applicable provisions of this Convention.

4. The provisions of this Article shall not apply in respect of any income paid under, or as part of, a conduit arrangement.

ARTICLE 23
Limitation on Benefits

1. Except as otherwise provided in this Article, a resident of a Contracting State that derives income, profits or gains from the other Contracting State shall be entitled to all the benefits of this Convention otherwise accorded to residents of a Contracting State only if such resident is a "qualified person" as defined in paragraph 2 of this Article and satisfies any other specified conditions for the obtaining of such benefits.

2. A resident of a Contracting State is a qualified person for a taxable or chargeable period only if such resident is either:

    a) an individual;

    b) a qualified governmental entity;

    c) a company, if

        (i) the principal class of its shares is listed or admitted to dealings on a recognized stock exchange specified in clauses (i) or (ii) of sub-paragraph a) of paragraph 7 of this Article and is regularly traded on one or more recognized stock exchanges, or

(ii) shares representing at least 50 per cent. of the aggregate voting power and value of the company are owned directly or indirectly by five or fewer companies entitled to benefits under clause (i) of this sub-paragraph, provided that, in the case of indirect ownership, each intermediate owner is a resident of either Contracting State;

d) a person other than an individual or a company, if:

(i) the principal class of units in that person is listed or admitted to dealings on a recognized stock exchange specified in clauses (i) or (ii) of sub-paragraph a) of paragraph 7 of this Article and is regularly traded on one or more recognized stock exchanges, or

(ii) the direct or indirect owners of at least 50 per cent. of the beneficial interests in that person are qualified persons by reason of clause (i) of sub-paragraph c) or clause (i) of this sub-paragraph;

e) a person described in sub-paragraph a), b) or c) of paragraph 3 of Article 4 (Residence) of this Convention, provided that, in the case of a person described in sub-paragraph a) or b) of that paragraph, more than 50 per cent. of the person's beneficiaries, members or participants are individuals who are residents of either Contracting State;

f) a person other than an individual, if:

(i) on at least half the days of the taxable or chargeable period persons that are qualified persons by reason of sub-paragraphs a), b), clause (i) of sub-paragraph c), clause (i) of sub-paragraph d), or sub-paragraph e) of this paragraph own, directly or indirectly, shares or other beneficial interests representing at least 50 per cent. of the aggregate voting power and value of the person, and

(ii) less than 50 per cent. of the person's gross income for that taxable or chargeable period is paid or accrued, directly or indirectly, to persons who are not residents of either Contracting State in the form of payments that are deductible for the purposes of the taxes covered by this Convention in the State of which the person is a resident (but not including arm's length payments in the ordinary course of business for services or tangible property and payments in respect of financial obligations to a bank, provided that where such a bank is not a resident of a Contracting State such payment is attributable to a permanent establishment of that bank located in one of the Contracting States); or

g) a trust or trustee of a trust in their capacity as such if at least 50 per cent. of the beneficial interest in the trust is held by persons who are either:

(i) qualified persons by reason of sub-paragraphs a), b), clause (i) of sub-paragraph c), clause (i) of sub-paragraph d), or sub-paragraph e) of this paragraph; or

(ii) equivalent beneficiaries,

provided that less than 50 per cent. of the gross income arising to such trust or trustee in their capacity as such for the taxable or chargeable period is paid or accrued, directly or indirectly, to persons who are not residents of either Contracting State in the form of payments that are deductible for the purposes of the taxes covered by this Convention in the Contracting State of which that trust or trustee is a resident (but not including arm's length payments in the ordinary course of business for services or tangible property and payments in respect of financial obligations to a bank, provided that where such a bank is not a resident of a Contracting State such payment is attributable to a permanent establishment of that bank located in one of the Contracting States).

3. Notwithstanding that a company that is a resident of a Contracting State may not be a qualified person, it shall be entitled to the benefits of this Convention otherwise accorded to residents of a Contracting State with respect to an item of income, profit or gain if it satisfies any other specified conditions for the obtaining of such benefits and:

a) shares representing at least 95 per cent. of the aggregate voting power and value of the company are owned, directly or indirectly, by seven or fewer persons who are equivalent beneficiaries; and

b) less than 50 per cent. of the company's gross income for the taxable or chargeable period in which the item of income, profit or gain arises is paid or accrued, directly or indirectly, to persons who are not equivalent beneficiaries, in the form of payments that are deductible for the purposes of the taxes covered by this Convention in the State of which the company is a resident (but not including arm's length payments in the ordinary course of business for services or tangible property and payments in respect of financial obligations to a bank, provided that where such a bank is not a resident of a Contracting State such payment is attributable to a permanent establishment of that bank located in one of the Contracting States).

4.   a) Notwithstanding that a resident of a Contracting State may not be a qualified person, it shall be entitled to the benefits of this Convention with respect to an item of income, profit or gain derived from the other Contracting State, if the resident is engaged in the active conduct of a trade or business in the first-mentioned State (other than the business of making or managing investments for the resident's own account, unless these activities are banking, insurance or securities activities carried on by a

bank, insurance company or registered securities dealer), the income, profit or gain derived from the other Contracting State is derived in connection with, or is incidental to, that trade or business and that resident satisfies any other specified conditions for the obtaining of such benefits.

b) If a resident of a Contracting State or any of its associated enterprises carries on a trade or business activity in the other Contracting State which gives rise to an item of income, profit or gain, sub-paragraph a) of this paragraph shall apply to such item only if the trade or business activity in the first-mentioned State is substantial in relation to the trade or business activity in the other State. Whether a trade or business activity is substantial for the purposes of this paragraph shall be determined on the basis of all the facts and circumstances.

c) In determining whether a person is engaged in the active conduct of a trade or business in a Contracting State under sub-paragraph a) of this paragraph, activities conducted by a partnership in which that person is a partner and activities conducted by persons connected to such person shall be deemed to be conducted by such person. A person shall be connected to another if one possesses at least 50 per cent. of the beneficial interest in the other (or, in the case of a company, shares representing at least 50 per cent. of the aggregate voting power and value of the company or of the beneficial equity interest in the company) or another person possesses, directly or indirectly, at least 50 per cent. of the beneficial interest (or, in the case of a company, shares representing at least 50 per cent. of the aggregate voting power and value of the company or of the beneficial equity interest in the company) in each person. In any case, a person shall be considered to be connected to another if, on the basis of all the facts and circumstances, one has control of the other or both are under the control of the same person or persons.

5. Notwithstanding the preceding provisions of this Article, if a company that is a resident of a Contracting State, or a company that controls such a company, has outstanding a class of shares:

a) which is subject to terms or other arrangements which entitle its holders to a portion of the income, profit or gain of the company derived from the other Contracting State that is larger than the portion such holders would receive in the absence of such terms or arrangements; and

b) 50 per cent. or more of the voting power and value of which is owned by persons who are not equivalent beneficiaries,

the benefits of this Convention shall apply only to that proportion of the income which those holders would have received in the absence of those terms or arrangements.

6. A resident of a Contracting State that is neither a qualified person nor entitled to benefits with respect to an item of income, profit or gain under paragraph 3 or 4 of this Article shall, nevertheless, be granted benefits of this Convention with respect to such item if the competent authority of the other Contracting State determines that the establishment, acquisition or maintenance of such resident and the conduct of its operations did not have as one of its principal purposes the obtaining of benefits under this Convention.

The competent authority of the other Contracting State shall consult with the competent authority of the first-mentioned State before refusing to grant benefits of this Convention under this paragraph.

7. For the purposes of this Article the following rules and definitions shall apply:

a) the term "recognized stock exchange" means:

(i) the NASDAQ System and any stock exchange registered with the U.S. Securities and Exchange Commission as a national securities exchange under the U.S. Securities Exchange Act of 1934;

(ii) the London Stock Exchange and any other recognised investment exchange within the meaning of the Financial Services Act 1986 or, as the case may be, the Financial Services and Markets Act 2000;

(iii) the Irish Stock Exchange, the Swiss Stock Exchange and the stock exchanges of Amsterdam, Brussels, Frankfurt, Hamburg, Johannesburg, Madrid, Milan, Paris, Stockholm, Sydney, Tokyo, Toronto and Vienna; and

(iv) any other stock exchange which the competent authorities agree to recognise for the purposes of this Article;

b)   (i) the term "principal class of shares" means the ordinary or common shares of the company, provided that such class of shares represents the majority of the voting power and value of the company. If no single class of ordinary or common shares represents the majority of the aggregate voting power and value of the company, the "principal class of shares" is that class or those classes that in the aggregate represent a majority of the aggregate voting power and value of the company;

(ii) the term "shares" shall include depository receipts thereof or trust certificates thereof;

c) the term "units" as used in sub-paragraph d) of paragraph 2 of this Article includes shares and any other instrument, not being a debt-claim, granting an entitlement to share in the assets or income of, or receive a distribution from, the person. The term "principal class of units" means the class of units which represents the majority of the value of the person. If no single class of units represents the majority of the value of the person, the "principal class of units" is those classes that in the aggregate represent the majority of the value of the person;

d) an equivalent beneficiary is a resident of a Member State of the European Community or of a European Economic Area state or of a party to the North American Free Trade Agreement but only if that resident:

      (i)   A) would be entitled to all the benefits of a comprehensive convention for the avoidance of double taxation between any Member State of the European Community or a European Economic Area state or any party to the North American Free Trade Agreement and the Contracting State from which the benefits of this Convention are claimed, provided that if such convention does not contain a comprehensive limitation on benefits article, the person would be a qualified person under paragraph 2 of this Article (or for the purposes of sub-paragraph g) of paragraph 2, under the provisions specified in clause (i) of that sub-paragraph) if such person were a resident of one of the Contracting States under Article 4 (Residence) of this Convention; and

      B) with respect to income referred to in Article 10 (Dividends), 11 (Interest) or 12 (Royalties) of this Convention, would be entitled under such convention to a rate of tax with respect to the particular class of income for which benefits are being claimed under this Convention that is at least as low as the rate applicable under this Convention; or

      (ii) is a company resident in a Member State of the European Community which is entitled under the provisions of any Directive of the European Community to receive the particular class of income for which benefits are being claimed under this Convention free of withholding tax.

e) For the purposes of paragraph 2 of this Article, the shares in a class of shares or the units in a class of units are considered to be regularly traded on one or more recognized stock exchanges in a chargeable or taxable period if the aggregate number of shares or units of that class traded on such stock exchange or exchanges during the twelve months ending on the day before the beginning of that taxable or chargeable period is at least six per cent. of the average number of shares or units outstanding in that class during that twelve-month period.

f) A body corporate or unincorporated association shall be considered to be an insurance company if its gross income consists primarily of insurance or reinsurance premiums and investment income attributable to such premiums.

ARTICLE 24
Relief from Double Taxation

1. In accordance with the provisions and subject to the limitations of the law of the United States (as it may be amended from time to time without changing the general principle hereof), the United States shall allow to a resident or citizen of the United States as a credit against the United States tax on income

a) the income tax paid or accrued to the United Kingdom by or on behalf of such citizen or resident; and

b) in the case of a United States company owning at least 10 per cent. of the voting stock of a company that is a resident of the United Kingdom and from which the United States company receives dividends, the income tax paid or accrued to the United Kingdom by or on behalf of the payer with respect to the profits out of which the dividends are paid.

For the purposes of this paragraph, the taxes referred to in sub-paragraph b) of paragraph 3 and in paragraph 4 of Article 2 (Taxes Covered) of this Convention shall be considered income taxes.

2. For the purposes of applying paragraph 1 of this Article,

a) subject to sub-paragraph b) of this paragraph, an item of gross income, as determined under the laws of the United States, derived by a resident of the United States that, under this Convention, may be taxed in the United Kingdom shall be deemed to be income from sources in the United Kingdom;

b) however, gains derived by an individual while that individual was a resident of the United States, that are taxed in the United States in accordance with this Convention, and that may also be taxed in the United Kingdom by reason only of paragraph 6 of Article 13 (Gains) of this Convention, shall be deemed to be gains from sources in the United States.

3. Notwithstanding the provisions of paragraph 1 of this Article, the amount of United Kingdom petroleum revenue tax allowable as a credit against United States tax shall be limited to the amount attributable to the United Kingdom source taxable income in the following way, namely:

a) the amount of United Kingdom petroleum revenue tax on income from the extraction of minerals from oil or gas wells in the United Kingdom to be allowed as a credit for a taxable year shall not exceed the amount, if any, by which the product of the maximum statutory United States tax rate applicable to a corporation for such taxable year and the amount of such income exceeds the amount of other United Kingdom tax on such income;

b) the amount of United Kingdom petroleum revenue tax on income from the extraction of minerals from oil or gas wells in the United Kingdom that is not allowable as a credit under sub-paragraph a) of this paragraph, shall be deemed to be income taxes paid or accrued in the two preceding or five succeeding taxable years, to the extent not deemed paid or accrued in a prior taxable year, and shall be allowable as a credit in the year in which it is deemed paid or accrued subject to the limitation in sub-paragraph a) of this paragraph;

c) the provisions of sub-paragraphs a) and b) of this paragraph shall apply separately, *mutatis mutandis*, to the amount of United Kingdom petroleum revenue tax on income from initial transportation, initial treatment and initial storage of minerals from oil or gas wells in the United Kingdom.

4. Subject to the provisions of the law of the United Kingdom regarding the allowance as a credit against United Kingdom tax of tax payable in a territory outside the United Kingdom (which shall not affect the general principle hereof):

a) United States tax payable under the laws of the United States and in accordance with this Convention, whether directly or by deduction, on profits, income or chargeable gains from sources within the United States (excluding, in the case of a dividend, United States tax in respect of the profits out of which the dividend is paid) shall be allowed as a credit against any United Kingdom tax computed by reference to the same profits, income or chargeable gains by reference to which the United States tax is computed;

b) in the case of a dividend paid by a company which is a resident of the United States to a company which is a resident of the United Kingdom and which controls directly or indirectly at least 10 per cent. of the voting power in the company paying the dividend, the credit shall take into account (in addition to any United States tax for which credit may be allowed under the provisions of sub-paragraph a) of this paragraph) the United States tax payable by the company in respect of the profits out of which such dividend is paid;

c) United States tax shall not be taken into account under sub-paragraph b) of this paragraph for the purpose of allowing credit against United Kingdom tax in the case of a dividend paid by a company which is a resident of the United States if and to the extent that

(i) the United Kingdom treats the dividend as beneficially owned by a resident of the United Kingdom; and

(ii) the United States treats the dividend as beneficially owned by a resident of the United States; and

(iii) the United States has allowed a deduction to a resident of the United States in respect of an amount determined by reference to that dividend;

d) the provisions of paragraph 2 of Article 1 (General Scope) of this Convention shall not apply to sub-paragraph c) of this paragraph.

For the purposes of this paragraph, the income taxes referred to in clause (i) of sub-paragraph a) of paragraph 3 and in paragraph 4 of Article 2 (Taxes Covered) of this Convention shall be considered United States tax.

5. For the purposes of paragraph 4 of this Article, profits, income and chargeable gains owned by a resident of the United Kingdom which may be taxed in the United States in accordance with this Convention shall be deemed to arise from sources within the United States.

6. Where the United States taxes, in accordance with paragraph 4 of Article 1 (General Scope) of this Convention, a United States citizen, or a former United States citizen or long-term resident, who is a resident of the United Kingdom:

a) the United Kingdom shall not be bound to give credit to such resident for United States tax on profits, income or chargeable gains from sources outside the United States as determined under the laws of the United Kingdom;

b) in the case of profits, income or chargeable gains from sources within the United States, the United Kingdom shall take into account for the purposes of computing the credit to be allowed under paragraph 4 of this Article only the amount of tax, if any, that the United States may impose under the provisions of this Convention on a resident of the United Kingdom who is not a United States citizen;

c) for the purposes of computing United States tax on the profits, income or chargeable gains referred to in sub-paragraph b) of this paragraph, the United States shall allow as a credit against United States tax the income tax and capital gains tax paid to the United Kingdom after the credit referred to in sub-paragraph b) of this paragraph; the credit so allowed shall not reduce the portion of the United States tax that is creditable against the United Kingdom tax in accordance with sub-paragraph b) of this paragraph; and

d) for the exclusive purpose of relieving double taxation in the United States under sub-paragraph c) of this paragraph, profits, income and chargeable gains referred to in sub-paragraph b) of this paragraph shall be deemed to arise in the United Kingdom to the extent necessary to avoid double taxation of such profits, income or chargeable gains under sub-paragraph c) of this paragraph.

ARTICLE 25

Non-Discrimination

1. Nationals of a Contracting State shall not be subjected in the other Contracting State to any taxation or any requirement connected therewith that is more burdensome than the taxation and connected requirements to which nationals of that other State in the same circumstances, particularly with respect to taxation on worldwide income, are or may be subjected.

2. The taxation on a permanent establishment that an enterprise of a Contracting State has in the other Contracting State shall not be less favourably levied in that other State than the taxation levied on enterprises of that other State carrying on the same activities.

3. Except where the provisions of the second sentence of paragraph 5 of Article 7 (Business Profits), paragraph 1 of Article 9 (Associated Enterprises), paragraph 9 of Article 10 (Dividends), paragraphs 4 and 7 of Article 11 (Interest), paragraphs 4 and 5 of Article 12 (Royalties), or paragraphs 3 and 4 of Article 22 (Other Income) of this Convention apply, interest, royalties, and other disbursements paid by a resident of a Contracting State to a resident of the other Contracting State shall, for the purpose of determining the taxable profits of the first-mentioned resident, be deductible under the same conditions as if they had been paid to a resident of the first-mentioned State.

4. Enterprises of a Contracting State, the capital of which is wholly or partly owned or controlled, directly or indirectly, by one or more residents of the other Contracting State, shall not be subjected in the first-mentioned State to any taxation or any requirement connected therewith that is more burdensome than the taxation and connected requirements to which other similar enterprises of the first-mentioned State are or may be subjected.

5. Nothing in this Article shall be construed as obliging either Contracting State to grant to individuals not resident in that State any of the personal allowances, reliefs and reductions for tax purposes which are granted to individuals so resident or to its nationals.

6. Nothing in this Article shall be construed as preventing either Contracting State from imposing a tax as described in paragraph 7 of Article 10 (Dividends) of this Convention.

7. The provisions of this Article shall, notwithstanding the provisions of Article 2 (Taxes Covered) of this Convention, also apply to taxes of every kind and description imposed by each Contracting State or by its political sub-divisions or local authorities.

ARTICLE 26

Mutual Agreement Procedure

1. Where a person considers that the actions of one or both of the Contracting States result or will result for him in taxation not in accordance with the provisions of this Convention, he may, irrespective of the remedies provided by the domestic law of those States,

present his case to the competent authority of the Contracting State of which he is a resident or national. The case must be presented within three years from the first notification of the action resulting in taxation not in accordance with the provisions of this Convention or, if later, within six years from the end of the taxable year or chargeable period in respect of which that taxation is imposed or proposed.

2. The competent authority shall endeavour, if the objection appears to it to be justified and if it is not itself able to arrive at a satisfactory solution, to resolve the case by mutual agreement with the competent authority of the other Contracting State, with a view to the avoidance of taxation which is not in accordance with this Convention. Any agreement reached shall be implemented notwithstanding any time limits or other procedural limitations in the domestic law of the Contracting States, except such limitations as apply for the purposes of giving effect to such an agreement.

3. The competent authorities of the Contracting States shall endeavour to resolve by mutual agreement any difficulties or doubts arising as to the interpretation or application of this Convention. In particular the competent authorities of the Contracting States may agree:

a) to the same attribution of income, deductions, credits, or allowances of an enterprise of a Contracting State to its permanent establishment situated in the other Contracting State;

b) to the same allocation of income, deductions, credits, or allowances between persons;

c) to the same characterization of particular items of income, including the same characterization of income that is assimilated to income from shares by the taxation law of one of the Contracting States and that is treated as a different class of income in the other Contracting State;

d) to the same characterization of persons;

e) to the same application of source rules with respect to particular items of income;

f) to a common meaning of a term;

g) that the conditions for the application of the second sentence of paragraph 5 of Article 7 (Business Profits), paragraph 9 of Article 10 (Dividends), paragraph 7 of Article 11 (Interest), paragraph 5 of Article 12 (Royalties), or paragraph 4 of Article 22 (Other Income) of this Convention are met; and

h) to the application of the provisions of domestic law regarding penalties, fines, and interest in a manner consistent with the purposes of this Convention.

They may also consult together for the elimination of double taxation in cases not provided for in this Convention.

4. The competent authorities of the Contracting States may communicate with each other directly for the purpose of reaching an agreement in the sense of the preceding paragraphs.

ARTICLE 27
Exchange of Information and Administrative Assistance

1. The competent authorities of the Contracting States shall exchange such information as is necessary for carrying out the provisions of this Convention or of the domestic laws of the Contracting States concerning taxes covered by this Convention insofar as the taxation thereunder is not contrary to this Convention, including for the purposes of preventing fraud and facilitating the administration of statutory provisions against legal avoidance. This includes information relating to the assessment or collection of, the enforcement or prosecution in respect of, or the determination of appeals in relation to, the taxes covered by this Convention. The exchange of information is not restricted by paragraph 1 of Article 1 (General Scope) of this Convention. Any information received by a Contracting State shall be treated as secret in the same manner as information obtained under the domestic laws of that State but may be disclosed to and only to persons or authorities (including courts and administrative bodies) involved in the assessment, collection, or administration of, the enforcement or prosecution in respect of, or the determination of appeals in relation to, the taxes covered by this Convention or the oversight of the above. Such persons or authorities shall use the information only for such purposes. They may disclose the information in public court proceedings or in judicial decisions.

2. If information is requested by a Contracting State in accordance with this Article, the other Contracting State shall obtain that information in the same manner and to the same extent as if the tax of the first-mentioned State were the tax of that other State and were being imposed by that other State, notwithstanding that the other State may not, at that time, need such information for the purposes of its own tax.

3. In no case shall the provisions of paragraphs 1 and 2 of this Article be construed so as to impose on a Contracting State the obligation:

a) to carry out administrative measures at variance with the laws and administrative practice of that or of the other Contracting State;

b) to supply information that is not obtainable under the laws or in the normal course of the administration of that or of the other Contracting State;

c) to supply information that would disclose any trade, business, industrial, commercial, or professional secret or trade process, or information the disclosure of which would be contrary to public policy.

4. If specifically requested by the competent authority of a Contracting State, the competent authority of the other Contracting State shall provide information under this Article in the form of authenticated copies of unedited original documents (including books, papers, statements, records, accounts, and writings), to the same extent such documents can be obtained under the laws and administrative practices of that other State with respect to its own taxes.

5. Each of the Contracting States shall endeavour to collect on behalf of the other Contracting State such amounts as may be necessary to ensure that relief granted by this Convention from taxation imposed by that other State does not inure to the benefit of persons not entitled thereto. This paragraph shall not impose upon either of the Contracting States the obligation to carry out administrative measures that would be contrary to its sovereignty, security, or public policy.

6. The competent authority of a Contracting State intending to send officials of that State to the other Contracting State to interview individuals and examine books and records with the consent of the persons subject to examination shall notify the competent authority of the other Contracting State of that intention.

7. The competent authorities of the Contracting States shall consult with each other for the purpose of co-operating and advising in respect of any action to be taken in implementing this Article.

ARTICLE 28

Diplomatic Agents and Consular Officers

Nothing in this Convention shall affect the fiscal privileges of diplomatic agents or consular officers under the general rules of international law or under the provisions of special agreements.

ARTICLE 29

Entry into Force

1. This Convention shall be subject to ratification in accordance with the applicable procedures of each Contracting State and instruments of ratification shall be exchanged as soon as possible.

2. This Convention shall enter into force upon the exchange of instruments of ratification and its provisions shall have effect:

a) in the United States:

(i) in respect of taxes withheld at source, for amounts paid or credited on or after the first day of the second month next following the date on which this Convention enters into force;

(ii) in respect of other taxes, for taxable periods beginning on or after the first day of January next following the date on which this Convention enters into force; and

b) in the United Kingdom:

(i) in respect of taxes withheld at source, for amounts paid or credited on or after the first day of the second month next following the date on which this Convention enters into force;

(ii) in respect of income tax not described in clause (i) of this sub-paragraph and capital gains tax, for any year of assessment beginning on or after the sixth day of April next following the date on which this Convention enters into force;

(iii) in respect of corporation tax, for any financial year beginning on or after the first day of April next following the date on which this Convention enters into force;

(iv) in respect of petroleum revenue tax, for chargeable periods beginning on or after the first day of January next following the date on which this Convention enters into force.

3. The Convention between the Government of the United States of America and the Government of the United Kingdom of Great Britain and Northern Ireland for the Avoidance of Double Taxation and the Prevention of Fiscal Evasion with Respect to Taxes on Income and Capital Gains, signed at London on December 31st, 1975, as modified by subsequent notes and protocols ("the prior Convention") shall cease to have effect in relation to any tax with effect from the date on which this Convention has effect in relation to that tax in accordance with paragraph 2 of this Article. Notwithstanding the preceding sentence, where any person entitled to benefits under the prior Convention would have been entitled to greater benefits thereunder than under this Convention, the prior Convention shall, at the election of such person, continue to have effect in its entirety with respect to that person for a twelve-month period from the date on which the provisions of this Convention otherwise would have effect under paragraph 2 of this Article. The prior Convention shall terminate on the last date on which it has effect in relation to any tax in accordance with the foregoing provisions of this paragraph.

4. Notwithstanding the entry into force of this Convention, an individual who is entitled to the benefits of Article 20 (Teachers) of the prior Convention at the time of the entry into force of this Convention shall continue to be entitled to such benefits until such time as the individual would have ceased to be entitled to such benefits if the prior Convention had remained in force.

5. Notwithstanding the entry into force of this Convention, an individual who is entitled to the benefits of Article 21 (Students and Trainees) of the prior Convention at the time of entry

into force of this Convention shall continue to be entitled to such benefits as if the prior Convention had remained in force.

ARTICLE 30
Termination

This Convention shall remain in force until terminated by a Contracting State. Either Contracting State may terminate this Convention by giving notice of termination to the other Contracting State through diplomatic channels. In such event, this Convention shall cease to have effect:

a) in the United States:

    (i) in respect of taxes withheld at source, for amounts paid or credited after the date that is six months after the date on which notice of termination was given; and

    (ii) in respect of other taxes, for taxable periods beginning on or after the date that is six months after the date on which notice of termination was given.

b) in the United Kingdom:

    (i) in respect of taxes withheld at source, for amounts paid or credited after the date that is six months after the date on which notice of termination was given;

    (ii) in respect of income tax not described in clause (i) of this sub-paragraph and capital gains tax, for any year of assessment beginning on or after the date that is six months after the date on which notice of termination was given;

    (iii) in respect of corporation tax, for any financial year beginning on or after the date that is six months after the date on which notice of termination was given; and

    (iv) in respect of petroleum revenue tax, for chargeable periods beginning on or after the date that is six months after the date on which notice of termination was given.

IN WITNESS WHEREOF, the undersigned, being duly authorised thereto by their respective Governments, have signed this Convention.

DONE at London in duplicate, this twenty-fourth day of July, 2001.

FOR THE GOVERNMENT OF
THE UNITED STATES OF AMERICA:

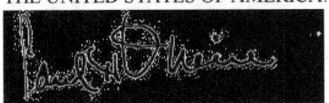

FOR THE GOVERNMENT OF
THE UNITED KINGDOM OF GREAT
BRITAIN AND NORTHERN IRELAND: